DRAWING
MANGA FACES
AND BODIES

ANNA SOUTHGATE AND YISHAN LI

rosen publishing's
rosen
central®

NEW YORK

This edition published in 2013 by:

The Rosen Publishing Group, Inc.
29 East 21st Street
New York, NY 10010

Additional end matter copyright © 2013 by The Rosen Publishing Group, Inc.

Library of Congress Cataloging-in-Publication Data

Southgate, Anna.
Drawing manga faces and bodies/Anna Southgate, Yishan Li.—First [edition].
      pages cm.—(Manga mania)
Includes bibliographical references and index.
ISBN 978-1-4488-9241-9 (library binding)—
ISBN 978-1-4488-9263-1 (pbk.)—
ISBN 978-1-4488-9264-8 (6-pack)
1. Face in art—Juvenile literature. 2. Human figure in art—Juvenile literature. 3. Comic books, strips, etc.—Japan—Technique—Juvenile literature. 4. Cartooning—Technique—Juvenile literature. I. Li, Yishan. II. Title.
NC1764.8.F33S685 2013
741.5'1—dc23

2012034786

Manufactured in the United States of America

CPSIA Compliance Information: Batch #W13YA: For further information, contact Rosen Publishing, New York, New York, at 1-800-237-9932.

All other content copyright © 2011 Axis Books Limited, London.

CONTENTS

Introduction 4

Chapter One
Manga Materials
and Equipment   **6**

Chapter Two
Expressions and Emotions   **18**

Chapter Three
Drawing Hairstyles   **25**

Chapter Four
Bodies and Poses   **35**

Chapter Five
Arms, Hands, and Fingers   **41**

Chapter Six
Legs, Feet, and Toes   **59**

Glossary 73

For More Information 74

For Further Reading 76

Index 78

INTRODUCTION

The art of manga grew from its origins in Japanese comic books to a worldwide phenomenon. Not only is it an art style, it's a way of life for some fans. So, how do you get started creating your own manga?

Perfecting any art style takes a lot of time, skill, and practice. But you can't perfect your style until you have the basics.

Bodies and faces are one of the most difficult things for artists to draw. How do you draw an angry or sad expression or capture what it really looks like when the sun shines on someone's hair? How can you make a character dance, run, or fight using only a writing utensil and piece of paper? This book can give you those basics.

First, you need the right tools. Then, you need to understand some basic drawing techniques. Finally, you just need a lot of practice. Once you master the basics of manga art, you will be ready to start creating characters with lives and actions of their own. While drawing can be extremely challenging at times and you'll go through plenty of erasers, stick with it. You'll never know what you will create!

Chapter One
Manga Materials and Equipment

There are several ways to produce manga art. You can draw and colour images by hand, generate them on a computer or work using a combination of both. Whichever style suits you, there are plenty of options when it comes to buying materials. This section of the book outlines the basics in terms of paper, pencils, inking pens, markers and paints, and will help you to make choices that work for you.

MANGA MATERIALS AND EQUIPMENT

Artists have their preferences when it comes to equipment, but regardless of personal favourites, you will need a basic set of materials that will enable you to sketch, ink and colour your manga art. The items discussed here are only a guide – don't be afraid to experiment to find out what works best for you.

PAPERS

You will need two types of paper – one for creating sketches, the other for producing finished colour artwork.

For quickly jotting down ideas, almost any piece of scrap paper will do. For more developed sketching, though, use tracing paper. Tracing paper provides a smooth surface, helping you to sketch freely. It is also forgiving – any mistakes can easily be erased several times over. Typically, tracing paper comes in pads. Choose a pad that is around 90gsm (24lb) in weight for best results – lighter tracing papers may buckle and heavier ones are not suitable for sketching. Once you have finished sketching out ideas, you will need to transfer them to the paper you want to produce your finished coloured art on. To do this, you will have to trace over your pencil sketch, so the paper you choose cannot be too opaque or heavy – otherwise you will not be able to see the sketch underneath. Choose a paper around 60gsm (16lb) for this. The type of paper you use is also important. If you are going to colour using marker pens, use marker or layout paper. Both of these types are very good at holding the ink found in markers. Other papers of the same weight can cause the marker ink to bleed, that is, the ink soaks beyond the inked lines of your drawing and produces fuzzy edges. This does not look good. You may wish to colour your art using other materials, such as coloured pencils or watercolours. Drawing paper is good for graphite pencil and inked-only art (such as that found in the majority of manga comic books),

Experiment with different papers to find the one that suits your style of drawing and colouring best. Watercolour papers can be ideal if you like using lots of wet colour like inks to render your manga.

while heavyweight watercolour papers hold wet paint and coloured inks and come in a variety of surface textures.

Again, don't be afraid to experiment: you can buy many types of papers in single sheets while you find the ones that suit your artwork best.

PENCILS

The next step is to choose some pencils for your sketches. Pencil sketching is probably the most important stage, and always comes first when producing manga art (you cannot skip ahead to the inking stage), so make sure you choose pencils that feel good in your hand and allow you to express your ideas freely.

Pencils are manufactured in a range of hard and soft leads. Hard leads are designated by the letter H and soft leads by the letter B. Both come in six levels – 6H is the hardest lead and 6B is the softest. In the middle is HB, a halfway mark between the two ranges. Generally, an HB and a 2B lead will serve most sketching purposes, with the softer lead being especially useful for loose, idea sketches, and the harder for more final lines.

Alternatively, you can opt for mechanical pencils. Also called self-propelling pencils, these come in a variety of lead grades and widths and never lose their point, making sharpening traditional wood-cased pencils a thing of the past. Whether you use one is entirely up to you

Graphite pencils are ideal for getting your ideas down on paper, and producing your initial drawing. The pencil drawing is probably the most important stage in creating your artwork. Choose an HB and a 2B to start with.

– it is possible to get excellent results whichever model you choose.

COLOURED PENCILS

Coloured pencils are effective and versatile colouring tools. A good box of pencils contains around 100 colours and will last for a long time, since a blunt pencil just needs sharpening, not replacing or refilling. Unlike with markers, successive layers of tone and shade can be built up with the same pencil, by gradually increasing the pressure on the pencil lead.

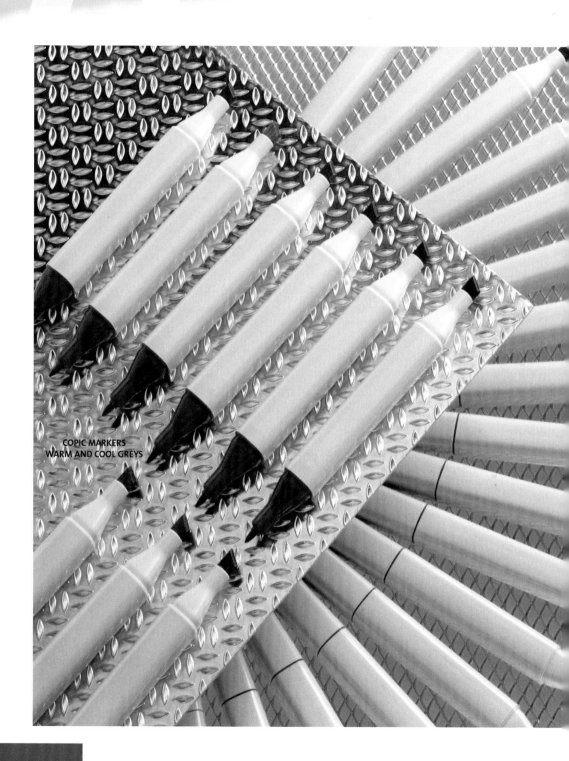

COPIC MARKERS
WARM AND COOL GREYS

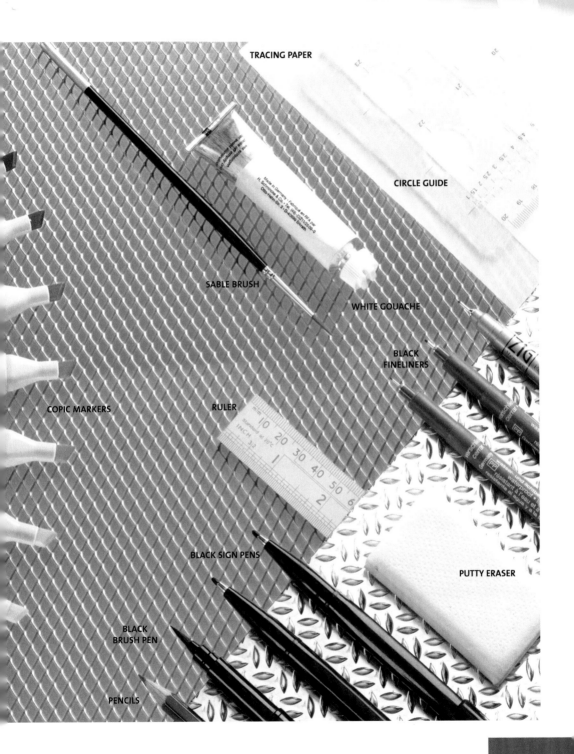

TRACING PAPER

CIRCLE GUIDE

SABLE BRUSH

WHITE GOUACHE

BLACK
FINELINERS

COPIC MARKERS

RULER

BLACK SIGN PENS

PUTTY ERASER

BLACK
BRUSH PEN

PENCILS

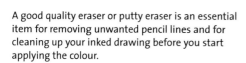

A good quality eraser or putty eraser is an essential item for removing unwanted pencil lines and for cleaning up your inked drawing before you start applying the colour.

Felt-tip pens are the ideal way to ink your sketches. A fineliner, medium-tip pen and sign pen should meet all of your needs, whatever your style and preferred subjects. A few coloured felt-tip pens can be a good addition to your kit, allowing you to introduce colour at the inking stage.

You can then build further colour by using a different colour pencil. Coloured pencils are also useful for adding detail, which is usually achieved by inking. This means that a more subtle level of detail can be achieved without having to ink in all lines. It is worth buying quality pencils. They do make a difference to the standard of your art and will not fade with age.

SHARPENERS AND ERASERS

If you use wooden pencils, you will need to get a quality sharpener; this is a small but essential piece of equipment. Electric sharpeners work very well and are also very fast; they last a long time too. Otherwise, a handheld sharpener is fine. One that comes with a couple of spare blades can be a worthwhile investment, to ensure that your pencils are always sharp. Along with a sharpener, you will need an eraser

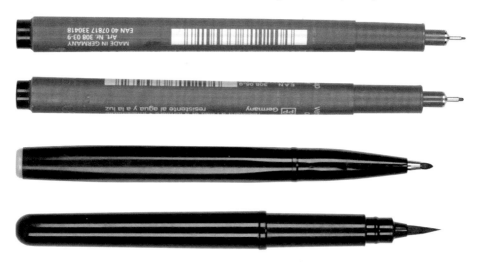

for removing any visible pencil lines from your inked sketches prior to colouring. Choose a high-quality eraser that does not smudge the pencil lead, scuff the paper, or leave dirty fragments all over your work. A soft putty eraser works best, since it absorbs pencil lead rather than just rubbing it away. For this reason, putty erasers do become dirty with use. Keep yours clean by trimming it carefully with scissors every now and then.

INKING PENS

The range of inking pens can be bewildering, but some basic rules will help you select the pens you need. Inked lines in most types of manga tend to be quite bold so buy a thin-nibbed pen, about 0.5mm, and a medium-size nib, about 0.8mm. Make sure that the ink in the pens is waterproof; this won't smudge or run. Next, you will need a medium-tip felt pen. Although you won't need to use this pen very often to ink the outlines of your characters, it is still useful for filling in small detailed areas of solid black. A Pentel pen does this job well. Last, consider a pen that can create different line widths according to the amount of pressure you put on the tip. These pens replicate brushes and allow you to create flowing lines such as those seen on hair and clothing. The Pentel brush pen does this very well, delivering a steady supply of ink to the tip from a replaceable cartridge. It is a good idea to test-drive a few pens at your art shop to see which ones suit you best. All pens should produce clean, sharp lines with a deep black pigment.

Markers come in a wide variety of colours, which allows you to achieve subtle variations in tone. In addition to a thick nib for broad areas of colour, the Copic markers shown here feature a thin nib for fine detail.

A selection of warm and cool greys is a useful addition to your marker colours and most ranges feature several different shades. These are ideal for shading on faces, hair, and clothes.

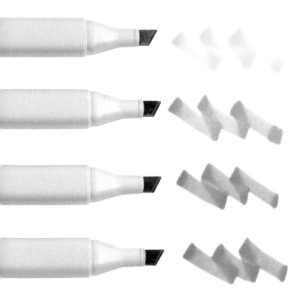

MARKERS AND COLOURING AIDS

Many artists use markers, rather than paint, to colour their artwork, because markers are easy to use and come in a huge variety of colours and shades. Good-quality markers, such as those made by Chartpak, Letraset or Copic, produce excellent, vibrant results, allowing you to build up multiple layers of colour so you can create rich, detailed work and precise areas of shading. Make sure that you use your markers with marker or layout paper to avoid bleeding. Markers are often refillable, so they last a long time. The downside is that they are expensive,

so choose a limited number of colours to start with, and add as your needs evolve. As always, test out a few markers in your art store before buying any.

However, markers are not the only colouring media. Paints and gouache also produce excellent results, and can give your work a distinctive look. Add white gouache, which comes in a tube, to your work to create highlights and sparkles of light. Apply it in small quantities with a good-quality watercolour brush. It is also possible to colour your artwork on computer. This is quick to do, although obviously there is a high initial outlay. It also tends to produce flatter colour than markers or paints.

DRAWING AIDS

Most of your sketching will be done freehand, but there are situations, especially with man-made objects such as the edges of buildings or the wheels of a car, when your line work needs to be crisp and sharp to create the right look.

If you are colouring with gouache or watercolour paint, then a selection of sizes of good quality sable watercolour brushes are invaluable.

Rulers, circle guides and compasses all provide this accuracy. Rulers are either metal or plastic; in most cases, plastic ones work best, though metal ones tend to last longer. For circles, use a circle guide, which is a plastic sheet with a wide variety of different-sized holes stamped out of it. If the circle you want to draw is too big for the circle guide, use a compass that can hold a pencil and inking pen.

If you want to draw manga comic strips, a pencil and a standard 30cm (12in) ruler are the only tools you will need to plan out your panels. (It is also possible to draw them digitally on computer.) Just remember to buy a quality ruler with an edge that will suit your pencils and pens and won't chip over time. A plastic one will generally last longer than a wooden one. Creating speech bubbles inside the panels is best done by hand, but templates are available if you need help. They do make your work look neat, they are generally cheap to buy, and they

Working freehand allows great freedom of expression and is ideal when you are working out a sketch, but you will find times when precision is necessary. Use compasses or a circle guide for circles and ellipses to keep your work sharp. Choose compasses that can be adjusted to hold both pencils and pens.

do not need replacing often. You can buy them in most art shops. It is possible to order authentic manga templates from Japan, but these are not really necessary unless you want to start collecting authentic manga art equipment. You can make your own templates out of cardboard if the ones in the shops do not suit your needs.

DRAWING BOARD

A drawing board is useful, since working on a flat table for a long time can give you a backache. Lots of different models are available, but all should be adjustable to the angle at which you want to work. They also come in a wide variety of sizes, from ones that sit on your lap or a tabletop to large work tables. If you do not want to invest in one immediately, it is possible to prop a piece of smooth, flat plywood about 60cm (24in) x 45cm (18in) on your desk. Put a small box underneath to create an angled surface.

A mannequin can be placed in different poses, helping you to visualise action and movement.

MANNEQUIN

A mannequin is an excellent tool for helping you to establish correct anatomical proportions, particularly for simpler poses such as walking and running. All the limbs are jointed to mimic human movement. They are also relatively cheap, but bear in mind that other reference materials may be necessary for more complicated movements, such as those involving martial arts. Photographic reference is often useful too.

USING A COMPUTER

When your sketches start coming easily and the more difficult features, such as texture and perspective, begin to look more convincing, you will be confident enough to expand on the range of scenes you draw. You might even begin to compose cartoon strips of your own or, at the very least, draw compositions in which several characters interact with each other – such as a battle scene.

Once you reach this stage, you might find it useful to start using a computer alongside your regular art materials. Used with a software program, like Adobe Photoshop, you can colour scanned-in sketches quickly and easily. You will also have a much wider range of colours to use, and can experiment at will. Moving one step further, a computer can save you a lot of time and energy when it comes to producing comic strips. Most software programs enable you to build a picture in layers. This means that you could have a general background layer – say a mountainous landscape – that always stays the same, plus a number of subsequent layers on

Once you have scanned your line artwork you can use computer programs, such as Adobe Photoshop, to colour your drawings and add some original material as well. The choice is a matter of personal preference. The speed of a computer makes adding colour to manga easy, once you have learnt the process.

which you can build your story. For example, you could use one layer for activity that takes place in the sky and another layer for activity that takes place on the ground. This means that you can create numerous frames simply by making changes to one layer, while leaving the others as they are. There is still a lot of work involved, but working this way does save you from having to draw the entire frame from scratch each time.

Of course, following this path means that you must invest in a computer if you don't already have one. You will also need a scanner and the relevant software. All of this can be expensive and it is worth getting your hand-drawn sketches up to a fairly accomplished level before investing too much money.

You can input a drawing straight into a computer program by using a graphics tablet and pen. The tablet plugs into your computer, much like a keyboard or mouse.

Chapter Two

Expressions and Emotions

FACIAL EXPRESSIONS

Once you have mastered basic face shape and features, you can have great fun giving your characters more expression. Depending on the scenario you are creating it pays to be able to portray a wide range of emotions as well as personal characteristics.

This sad boy has mournful eyes with heavy lids and downward-sloping eyebrows. The corners of his mouth also turn down.

This boy is crying with laughter. His eyes are closed and eyebrows raised. They mirror the open-mouthed smile.

A small, tight-lipped smile shows a serene happiness. The softly rounded eyebrows echo the curves of the bright eyes.

There is real anger here. All of the features are flared and angular. The eyebrows and facial lines show a tight expression.

With tears streaming down his face this boy's eyes are heavy and looking down. Straight lips and eyebrows convey sadness.

This boy looks anguished or alarmed. His mouth is part open, as if exclaiming or shouting, and his brow is furled.

ANNOYED MAN

This man's features are exaggerated so that the eyes and mouth are open wide, but angular rather than round. His knitted eyebrows arch steeply at the corners and his jaw is square. The hair pulled back away from the face makes the man's expression all the more severe.

This is a three-quarter view. Start with your pencil guides and begin to sketch in a basic outline of the man's face.

Note the man's angular profile. The wide-open mouth fills the bottom third of the face and the eyebrow stretches up to the hair.

Draw in the man's hairline across the forehead. Emphasise his annoyance by making the pupils in his eyes small and narrow.

Refine the outline of the hair and begin to work more on the mouth. The stretched lips are barely visible, all teeth are bared.

Add shadow in the mouth, giving shape to the tongue, and draw in the bottom teeth. Draw in the eyebrows and the cheekbones.

Go over your artwork in ink and colour the image. The light is coming from the left, so any shading should be at the rear.

HAPPY GIRL

Closed eyes and a smiling mouth are one of the simplest ways to convey happiness in manga art. Facial features are generally small and basic. The girl's soft, flowing blonde hair emphasises her benign appearance.

Start with pencil guides and sketch in a basic outline of the girl's face and hair. She is young, so her face is soft and rounded.

Draw outlines of her features, which will remain little changed. Her eyes sit on the horizontal guide, her nose is slight.

Work on the hair. It is thick and shoulder length. The tresses are heavy looking with a slight wave. She has a deep fringe.

Draw in more detail on the ear, keeping it simple so that it complements the other features. Finalise the shape of the mouth.

Draw feint lines above the eyes to suggest eyelids. Add a couple wrinkles to emphasise that the eyes are smiling. Add teeth.

Go over your artwork in ink and colour the image. Keep your colours flat. Work in darker tones for the shaded areas.

ANGRY GIRL

From the upward-sloping eyes and eyebrows, to the square lines of the mouth and jaw, to the pointed chin and shaggy hair, everything about this girl's expression is spiky. Her angry look completely fills her face.

Start with pencil guides and sketch in a basic outline of the girl's face and hair. Keep your lines simple at this stage.

Draw in the angled features. Rounded at the bottom, the eyes rise sharply from the centre of the face, as do the eyebrows.

Add narrow pupils and spiky eyelashes to emphasise the angry look. Begin to draw the uneven lengths of hair.

Finish the eyes and start to work on the mouth. This girl is shouting: her tongue and top teeth are visible.

Go over your drawing in ink and work in dark areas of shade in the mouth and below the chin. Erase any unwanted pencil lines.

Add colour to your drawing, paying close attention to the direction of the light. Use flat colours before adding shadow.

EVIL EXPRESSION

You can have a great deal of fun making evil characters, as they can be less human-looking than others. You can exaggerate their features, if you like, to make them look other-worldly. The trick with an evil expression is to use short, sharp, straight lines.

Begin with your pencil guide and draw a basic outline of the face. Keep the size small and neat. Draw a few sweeping hair lines.

Add facial features. Here they are stretched out to make them long and narrow, emphasizing the character's evil streak.

Draw the man's hair. Use short, straight lines to give him a spiked fringe and pull it back and away at the rear.

Finish by adding minor details to the ear, making it more pointed than usual if you like. Mark lines on his neck for more definition.

Go over your drawing in ink and erase any unwanted pencil lines. Use the ink to draw out the corners of the mouth.

Add colour to your drawing, keeping it flat and simple. The man has a pale complexion and there is minimal shading.

GALLERY

The key to creating convincing manga characters with a range of expressions lies in being able to draw the facial features accurately. The eyes are always important, but you can also convey different emotions and characteristics through the mouth, face shape and hair style.

hateful
right This character is beyond reason. His wide, frowning featureless eyes and square blaring mouth suggest real anger and intimidation.

angry
below This boy's short spiky hair emphasises his aggressive facial expression. The colours are cold.

serene
left This girl has soft straight lilac hair. Her eyes are closed as if in contemplation. The whole look is one of calm.

dreaming
below This character has a dreamy, faraway expression. Her benign look is emphasised by the girly hair accessory.

doubtful
right The look on this boy's face is one of uncertainty. His eyes and eyebrows are arched in a sideways quizzical look.

playful

right This character has a softness to him, and a boyish charm. He has bright but gentle eyes and a playful smile.

forlorn

above The downward looking eyes and slim downturned mouth belie a sadness that is only emphasised by the lank loose-hanging hair.

surprised

left This girl is gasping in surprise. Both her mouth and her huge, wide-open eyes have a slight downward look to them.

disappointment

right There is disbelief in this girl's expression, as if she is facing a great disappointment. She opens her mouth to speak, but cannot find the words.

hurt

above Someone has wronged this character and she is looking downcast and hurt. Frowning eyebrows and a quivering mouth emphasise the look.

Chapter Three

Drawing Hairstyles

DRAWING CURLY HAIR

The most important aspect of drawing curly hair is making it look three-dimensional, and there are two ways of achieving this. The first is to keep your ink drawing simple, allowing the lines to spiral and overlap in places. The second is to use different tones when it comes to adding colour.

For a loose curl, start with a simple wavy line. Keep it vertical and vaguely S-shaped. This marks an outside edge of the curl.

Draw a second wavy line a short way from the first, exaggerating the curves slightly. This marks the other outside edge.

Build on the curl by adding a few more wavy lines. Echo the shape of the first two lines, without overlapping them too closely.

Draw the lines a little closer together towards the end of the curl. See how the hair begins to look more realistic.

Go over your drawing in ink and add some feint lines for more detail. These will act as guides when it comes to adding colour.

Apply a flat colour to your work. Use your guidelines to add the darker tones that emphasise the shape of the curls.

PUTTING IT TOGETHER

Start with a basic outline of the hair. This style is shoulder length, with a deep fringe. Use a few soft lines to capture the shape.

Work on the individual curls by adding soft, wavy lines that intertwine and overlap with those of the initial outline.

Continue to build on the hair in this way. When it comes to the fringe, keep your lines simple and sweeping in the same direction.

Work on the ends of the curls, giving each a more defined shape. Draw a few feint lines to mark the crown of the head.

Add any final details – such as the curls that obscure the ear and go over your drawing in ink. Erase any unwanted pencil lines.

Colour your artwork, using flat colour initially. Your darker tones should follow your ink lines in order to emphasise the curls.

DRAWING RINGLETS

This is a very stylised look, principally for female characters. The idea is to draw each individual tress as a tight, spiralling ringlet. Once you have practised this a few times, you will have no trouble getting the ringlets to look uniform in size and shape.

Start with two roughly parallel lines. They do not have to be dead straight, but should follow a slight curve instead.

Now mark even sections down the length of your artwork, giving them a diagonal slant from left to right.

Modify your parallel lines, stepping them on the inside edge of the tress and rounding them more on the outside edge.

With your basic ringlets drawn, add a number of feint lines in each one to suggest individual hairs running through them.

Go over your drawing in ink and give more shape to the very last ringlet at the bottom. Erase any unwanted pencil lines.

Colour your image. Note how the shading is achieved using very subtle tones to make the ringlet round and three-dimensional.

PUTTING IT TOGETHER

Start with a very basic pencil outline of the shoulder-length hair and deep fringe. You just need a suggestion of the shape.

Draw in pairs of parallel lines – one pair per ringlet of hair. They should frame the girl's face at the sides.

With the ringlets drawn, start to mark the diagonal lines. Note that they slope in opposite directions either side of the head.

Modify the parallel lines of each tress. Remember that the inside edges are stepped. Draw in the thick, curved fringe.

Go over your drawing in ink and work in the many feint lines that suggest the individual hairs running through the tresses.

Colour your artwork. Use a strong flat colour before working in the darker tones. Try to make it look three-dimensional.

DRAWING WAVY HAIR

This is not all that different from the curly hair on pages 25–26. There is less volume here, which is achieved by making the curls in the wavy lines a little shallower. This is a style that can be used to great effect on both male and female characters.

For a single tress, start with a simple wavy line. Keep it roughly vertical, but draw in a couple of soft squiggles.

Draw a second wavy line next to the first. Follow the shape of the soft squiggles without repeating them exactly.

The idea is to draw a single tress that looks twisted here and there down its length. Your lines need to meet at a point at the bottom.

Continue to add similarly shaped lines to build up the volume of the tress. Don't overdo it – you want to achieve soft waves.

Go over your drawing in ink and add some feint lines for more detail. These will act as guides when it comes to adding colour.

Apply a flat colour to your work. Use your guidelines to add the darker tones that emphasise the wavy nature of the hair.

PUTTING IT TOGETHER

Start with a basic outline of the hair as it frames the top of the boy's head. The outline follows the oval guide closely.

Draw the outline of the deep fringe and of the longer hair at the back of the neck, which is roughly shoulder length.

Add further lines that mirror the shapes of the ones drawn in the previous step. Remember to bring them to a point at the end.

Continue to work in this way, building and better defining the individual tresses of wavy hair. Use the fringe to frame the face.

Go over your drawing in ink and erase any unwanted pencil lines. Add a few feint lines for a more detailed finish.

Colour your artwork. Use a flat colour of your choice. Add darker tones and subtle highlights to emphasise soft waves.

DRAWING HIGHLIGHTS

Highlights can be used to dramatic effect on any hairstyle of any colour. There are two things to remember. The first is that highlights need to reflect the direction from which the light is coming. The second is that they are most likely to feature on curved shapes.

left Here, the girl's hair as been coloured black. At the moment it is a uniform, flat colour and, as such, does not look very realistic.

right Very bright highlights show how the curved fringe catches the light. The bold strokes capture the glossy nature of the thick hair.

left The direction of light has shifted slightly and is, perhaps, less intense. See how the highlights are evenly distributed across the top of the head, as if the light is from above.

right The girl's hair is now almost exclusively white, drawn in bands radiating from the crown. This is useful for drawing the hair of older characters.

31

BLACK HAIR *COMPLEX HIGHLIGHTS*

Having established how to draw basic highlights, it pays to know how to render more complex highlights so that they look realistic. The key for all hair colours is to start with a flat colour of a middling tone. This way, you can build on the look by adding both lighter and darker shades.

It is a good idea to practise on a trial area first. For black hair, start with a flat wash of a dark-grey tone. Now use black for the

shaded areas, filling blocks of colour as well as drawing finer lines to suggest individual strands of hair. Complete the

effect using white for highlights in the same way. Use the natural curves as guides and consider the direction of the light.

PUTTING IT TOGETHER

Start with a mid-tone grey. Use this to fill the hair as a solid area of flat colour. Keep it as uniform as possible.

The light is from the left. Use solid black towards the rear of the head and under the fringe, graduating as you come forward.

Use bold, jagged lines for the white highlights. Note how they follow the curve of the fringe for a more realistic finish.

BLONDE HAIR *COMPLEX HIGHLIGHTS*

Highlights on blonde hair work in pretty much the same way as those for black. And, as long as you use two tones of the same colour, plus white, you will be able to create complex highlights for any of the lighter hair colours you choose, from sky blue to lilac and lemon yellow to pink.

Practise on a trial area. For blonde or pastel-coloured hair, start with a flat wash of a mid-tone. Now use a darker tone for

the shaded areas, filling blocks of colour as well as drawing finer lines to suggest individual strands of hair. Complete the

effect using white for highlights in the same way. Use the natural curves as guides and consider the direction of the light.

PUTTING IT TOGETHER

Start with a mid-tone yellow. Use this to fill the hair as a solid area of flat colour. Keep it as uniform as possible.

The light is from the left. Use dark yellow towards the rear of the head and under the fringe, graduating as you come forward.

The highlights follow the curve of the fringe as it catches the light. Use bold, jagged lines to render these realistically.

GALLERY

When considering a hairstyle for a manga character, it is not only important to think about gender, but also age, personality, status and profession. The most successful drawings will be those in which the hair appropriately complements such characteristics.

neat bun

right A neat bun at the back of the head, or one on each side, can be worn by young female characters. The look is not out of place in a dance studio or arty environment.

jaunty ponytail

above A high ponytail tied at the side would suit a fun, youthful character, like a waitress or student.

simple styling

left This simple cut, with centre parting, is perhaps suitable for a young office worker or teacher.

dressed up

right This look requires a little more effort to style and might be reserved for special occasions – say a party or hot date.

fun and funky

above This is best used on a young woman and might suit someone who plays in a band.

Chapter Four
Bodies and Poses

Once you are able to draw male and female figures accurately, you will find yourself inventing all kinds of stories for them. This section of the book looks at proportion and poses. It demonstrates how manga bodies vary and shows how to draw all manner of poses from standing and sitting to running, dancing and kicking a football. Armed with the basics, it will not be long before you are creating poses of your own.

SEATED FEMALE

This is quite a typical female pose, halfway between sitting and kneeling on the floor. It is suitable for young girls and early teens, who tend to be more supple.

Use a pencil to sketch a basic structure. The upper body is straightforward, but you really have to think about the positions of the girl's legs.

Use simple geometric shapes to draw the body parts, linking them together at the joints with circles or ovals. Think about perspective.

Use this structure to draw a solid outline. Think about the girl's muscular make-up as you do this. Draw in the guides for positioning facial features.

Draw in the girl's eyes and an outline of her hair. Give more shape to her body, drawing her chest more accurately.

Work on the abdomen now, adding a feint line to mark the ribcage. Give more shape to the legs and arms. Consider the perspective again.

Once you are happy with your pencil drawing, go over just the outline of the girl's body in ink. Take care to follow your sketch accurately.

Now draw the girl's clothes, using pencil. Her outfit is simple. You need only draw an outline, which you can then go over in ink.

Now you can add colour to your drawing. Use flat colour to start with. You can then build on the areas of light and shade.

GALLERY

Once you have mastered the few basic poses demonstrated on the previous pages you can start to broaden your catalogue of designs. Experiment with poses of all kinds so that you can build stories around your characters. Always think carefully about perspective.

standing pose

below Seen from a three-quarter view from the rear, this girl's physique is somewhat exaggerated. Her back has a pronounced arch.

kick boxer

right There is real power and energy in this pose. The girl's legs are dead straight, showing just how strong they are, and she has a muscular torso.

kneeling pose

right This is a neat, compact pose, with the feet comfortably tucked beneath the bottom. Perspective is key here.

GALLERY

While a number of poses suit only men or just women, the vast majority can be adapted for either gender. The main things to consider are proportion and build. Men generally tend to be leaner (if skinny) or more muscular (if well-built) than women.

resentment
right This boy is cross about something. He is sitting with his knees drawn up and his arms folded in determination.

bashful
below Leaning back slightly, and with her hands held behind her back, this girl looks shy. Her inclined head and turned-in feet emphasise the look.

anguish
below There is a tense anxiety in this girl's face that is reflected in her pose. Her back is rigid and her hands clenched.

sullen
above There is no tension in this seated pose. The boy's shoulders are sagging and his arms drape across his legs.

Chapter Five
Arms, Hands, and Fingers

It can be challenging to draw hands and arms convincingly. Hands are particularly difficult, because they make awkward shapes when they change position. In this section of the book, you will learn how to draw hands and arms in a range of poses and from a variety of different viewpoints. Once mastered, you can adapt these examples to come up with poses of your own design.

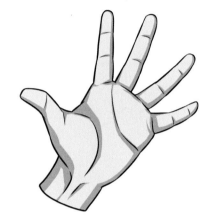

ARMS NATURAL POSE

This is the simplest pose for the arms – hanging down by the sides of the body. Follow the steps on pages 44 and 46 respectively for the open palm pose or clenched fist.

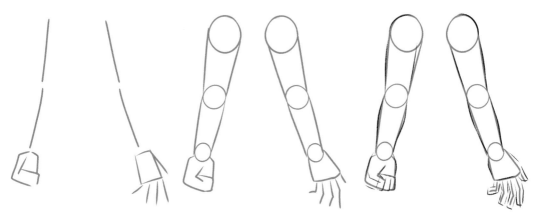

Start with a very simple pencil sketch. Draw straight lines as guides for the arms, and the first step for each hand pose.

Draw the arms as simple geometric shapes, linked at the joints by circles. Continue to work on the hands.

Use your guide to develop the shape of the arms to make them more realistic. These are quite muscular masculine arms.

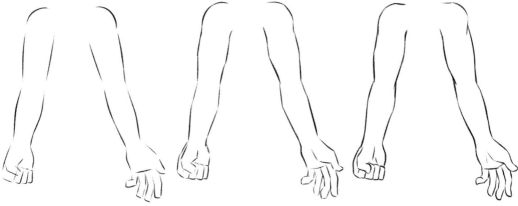

Turn you attention to the hands. Start to work on the perspective of the clenched fist and define the palm of the open hand.

Continue to work on the hands, rounding off the tips of the fingers and thumbs. Make sure their relative sizes are true.

Work your way up the arms, developing a more realistic shape – narrow at the wrists and elbows and rounded shoulders.

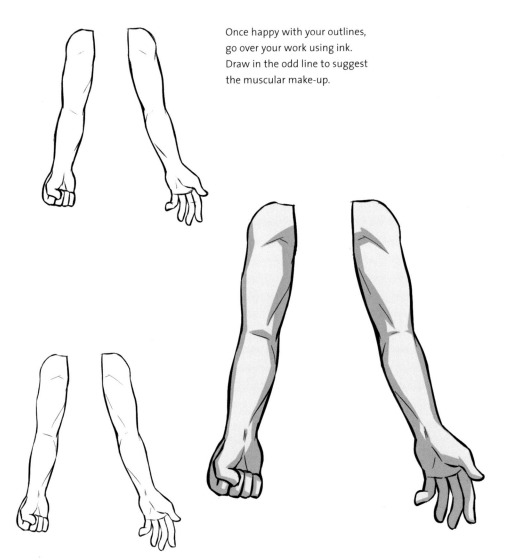

Once happy with your outlines, go over your work using ink. Draw in the odd line to suggest the muscular make-up.

You are now ready to colour your image. Add any finishing details in ink and erase unwanted pencil lines.

Colour your image. Choose a lifelike skin tone for a flat wash. Use a darker tone to emphasise the shapes of the muscles.

PAINTING NAILS

This is quite a complicated image. Not only do both hands have different poses (based on the open palm, page 44, and the fingers picking up, page 48), but the arms are crossed in front of the body and foreshortened. Getting the perspective right is key here.

Start with a basic structural sketch using pencil. Think very carefully about the positions of the arms and the shapes the hands are making.

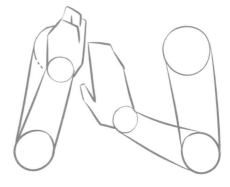

Draw the arms as simple geometric shapes, noting that the forearms are foreshortened. Use circles for the joints. Modify the shapes of the hands.

Use your guide to develop the shape of the arms to make them more realistic. They are quite feminine. Draw in each of the fingers and thumbs.

Continue to work on the hands, making sure that the perspective is working. The hand with the nail polish needs to appear slightly further back.

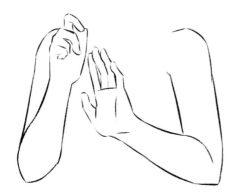

Round off the tips of the fingers and thumbs. Bend one or two of the fingers to give them a more realistic pose.

Add fingernails, knuckles and palm details. Draw in the nail polish. Work your way up the arms, giving them more shape.

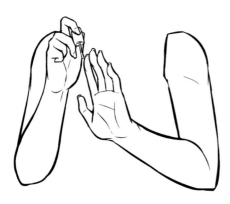

You are now ready to colour your image. Add any finishing details in ink and erase the unwanted pencil lines.

Colour your image. Choose a lifelike skin tone for a flat wash. Use a darker tone in the shaded areas so that your image looks three-dimensional.

LIFTING WEIGHTS

This pose is not dissimilar to the natural pose on pages 49–50. It is reasonably straightforward in that the arms are seen face on and are raised up above the head. The difference here is that the arms are in tension, and not relaxed, so are much more muscular.

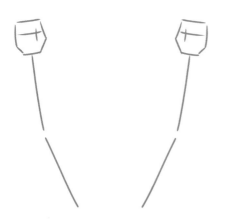

Start with a very simple pencil sketch. Draw straight lines as guides for the arms, and the first step for the hands in a fist pose (page 46).

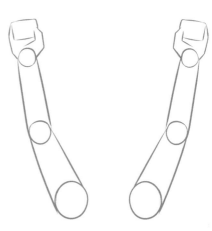

Draw the arms as simple geometric shapes, linked at the joints by circles. Draw the hands in more detail, giving them thumbs.

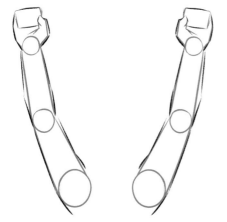

Use your guide to develop the shape of the arms to make them more realistic. They are very muscular and should be quite broad at the shoulders.

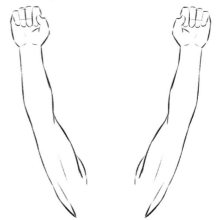

Start to establish the tense muscles, using a few lines to capture them bulging beneath the skin. Give more shape to the hands.

Work more detail into the palms of the hands and to the knuckles. Once happy with your outlines, go over your work using ink.

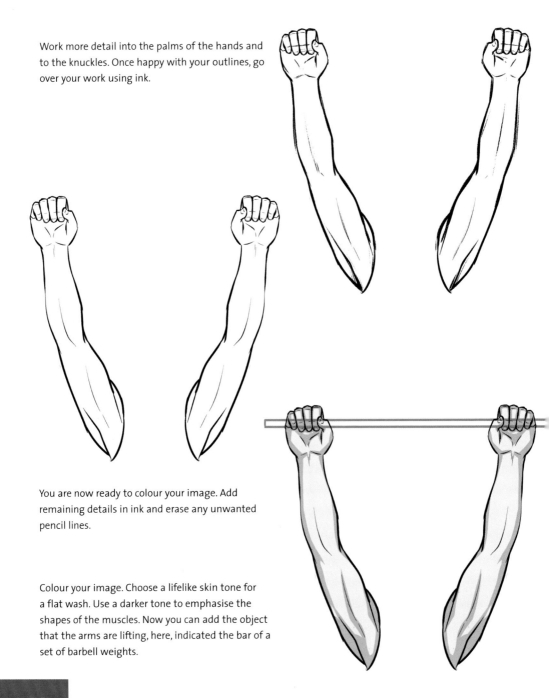

You are now ready to colour your image. Add remaining details in ink and erase any unwanted pencil lines.

Colour your image. Choose a lifelike skin tone for a flat wash. Use a darker tone to emphasise the shapes of the muscles. Now you can add the object that the arms are lifting, here, indicated the bar of a set of barbell weights.

PRAYING

This is a simple pose, with arms bent at the elbows and the hands clasped in prayer. It is worth having a photographic reference for getting the overlapping of the fingers correct, but the rest is pretty straightforward.

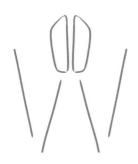

Start with a very simple pencil sketch. Draw straight lines as guides for the arms, and geometric shapes for the hands.

Build up the arms as simple geometric shapes, linked at the joints by circles. Refine the shapes of the hands.

Use your guide to develop the shape of the arms to make them more realistic. Note that this pose is quite symmetrical.

Continue to develop the shape of the arms to make them more realistic. These are the arms of a female character.

Take your time with the hands. Consider how the hands are clasped – loosely – and give more shape to the fingers.

Round off the fingertips, double checking that the fingers are the right length relative to one another. Keep them relaxed.

Draw in fingernails to make the hands look three-dimensional. Once happy with your outlines, go over your work using ink.

You are now ready to colour your image. Add any last details in ink and erase unwanted pencil lines.

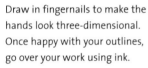

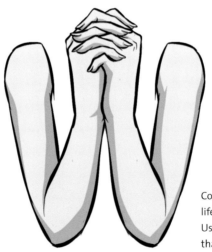

Colour your image. Choose a lifelike skin tone for a flat wash. Use a darker tone for the areas that are in shade.

GALLERY

Armed with the basics outlined in this chapter, you will soon be able to draw realistic hands and arms, keeping them three-dimensional and in perspective. They are never easy to draw, however, so try to find a good number of visual references to help you.

clenched fist

right Here is a view of the fist shown on page 46, but now seen from behind. Only the knuckles of the fingers and thumb are visible.

dancing arm

below The raised arm of a young character. The hand is relaxed and has the suggestion of movement, maybe dancing.

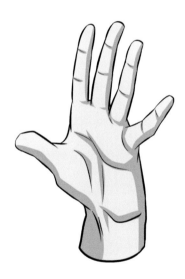

crawling fingers

below A youthful arm and hand, the fingers walking slowly across a surface. There could be something a little sinister about the pose.

relaxed arm

below Although similar to the image to the left, this is more relaxed. It might suit a character going somewhere in a hurry.

reaching for help

above This is a version of the open palm on page 44. There is a slight tension here, however, suggesting that the character is reaching out for help or grasping at something just beyond reach.

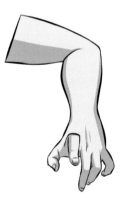

beckoning fingers

below A female hand making a beckoning gesture. The success of this pose lies in the accurate foreshortening of the hand.

keyboard fingers

above This hand is almost horizontal, with the fingers poised. It is a pose that could suit someone using a computer or playing the piano.

grabbing fingers

right Note the foreshortening of this outstretched hand. The fingers are bent in a grabbing motion and are about to pick something up.

hanging loose

right This is the pose of a very relaxed arm. The limb is hanging straight down and the fingers are curled towards the palm, but not clenched tight.

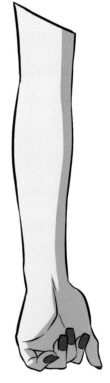

grasping fingers

above You can just imagine a tennis racket in the hand of this character. The positioning of the fingers suggests that, or something similar.

Chapter Six
Legs, Feet, and Toes

Legs and feet pose similar problems to hands and arms when it comes to drawing them. You need to have a good grip of perspective in order to capture them in a range of different poses. This section of the book offers instruction on drawing legs and feet from different viewpoints and in a range of activities. Having practised these, you'll soon be developing convincing poses of your own making.

LEG ANATOMY

In order to draw legs accurately, it helps to know a little bit about the human body. The success of your image relies on having some knowledge of the skeletal and muscular structure beneath the skin. This is true for all body parts – arms, legs, torso and so on.

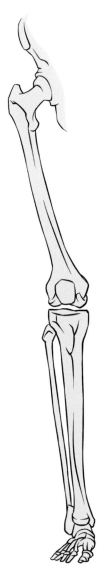

left The skeletal make-up of the leg, from hip to toe. You can see the bone structure of the limbs, as well as the correct proportions of thigh to shin – pretty much equal. You can also see the complicated joints at the hip, knee and ankle.

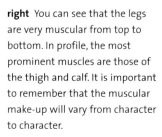

right You can see that the legs are very muscular from top to bottom. In profile, the most prominent muscles are those of the thigh and calf. It is important to remember that the muscular make-up will vary from character to character.

FOOT SIDE VIEW

The foot seen from the side is one of the easiest poses to draw, as long as you can get perspective and proportions right. You need to consider the relative sizes of the toes, but also the fact that they recede into the distance.

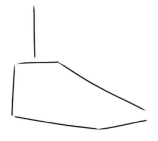

Draw an outline using pencil. Use a simple geometric shape for the foot and mark the approximate position of the ankle.

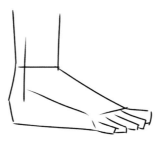

Work on the perspective. Divide the foot shape into sections for the side and top of the foot. Mark out each toe.

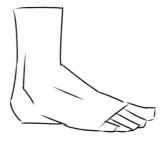

Give more shape to the sole of the foot. Round off the heel and sculpt the arch. Define the ankle bone a little more clearly.

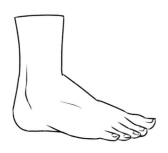

Work on the toes, paying attention to their relative sizes. Draw in the toenails. Go over your drawing in ink.

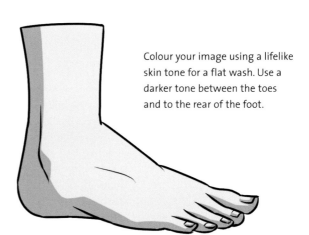

Colour your image using a lifelike skin tone for a flat wash. Use a darker tone between the toes and to the rear of the foot.

FOOT FRONT VIEW

This is quite a difficult viewpoint to master, but a very useful one, as you will need it for any characters seen from the front. You will also need to adapt this version for the various stages of walking – mid-step, for example, where just the ball of the foot makes contact with the ground.

Start with a pencil outline. Draw the foot as a simple geometric form. Try to capture the basic shape the heel and toes make.

Make your drawing three-dimensional. Draw in the shin and ankle, then work on the heel section and each individual toe.

Give more shape to the toes now, curving the tips and marking out the joints. Work on the profile of the foot to define the ankle.

Finish the toes, giving them toenails, before going over your drawing in ink. Erase any unwanted pencil lines.

Now you can colour your image. Choose a lifelike skin tone for a flat wash. Use a darker tone in the shaded areas to the rear.

FOOT FROM BELOW

This is a useful viewpoint to master, as it can come in very handy when drawing characters who are mid-air for some reason – say you want to draw someone running or playing a sport, or even locked in combat with an enemy.

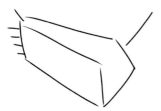

Draw an outline using pencil. Use a simple geometric shape for the foot and mark the approximate position of the ankle and toes.

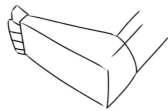

Make your drawing three-dimensional. Draw in the shin and ankle, then work on each individual toe.

Give more shape to the sole of the foot now, rounding the heel and marking the ball of the foot. Round off the toes nicely.

Add any final details – say the ankle bone – before going over your drawing in ink. Erase any unwanted pencil lines.

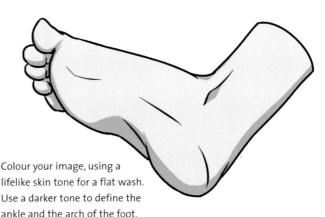

Colour your image, using a lifelike skin tone for a flat wash. Use a darker tone to define the ankle and the arch of the foot.

RUNNING

For this version of legs and feet, and for many others, the success lies in being able to show the action realistically. You may find it useful to find a drawing or photograph to refer to as you work.

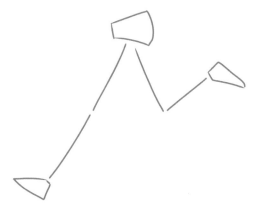

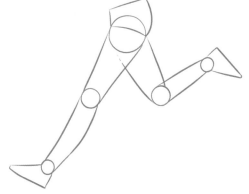

Start with a basic structural sketch using pencil. Draw the legs as straight lines for now, and use geometric shapes for the hips and feet.

Build on your structural sketch, drawing geometric shapes for each of the limbs. Link these at the joints using circles.

Use your guide to develop the shape of the legs to make them more realistic. They are working hard so their muscular make-up should be evident.

Continue to work on the outline, checking that the perspective is working. The side view means that one leg is partly obscured by the other.

Start to work on some of the finer details. Give more shape to the pelvic area and draw some feint lines to suggest muscles beneath the skin.

Add any final details – mark the ankle bones, for example – then go over your drawing in ink. Erase any unwanted pencil lines.

Use pencil to draw in the runner's shorts. These are tight-fitting and simply drawn using a couple of lines across the mid-thigh area.

Colour your image. Choose a lifelike skin tone for a flat wash. Note the direction of light when adding darker tones.

JUMPING

With this example, it is important to try to capture the movement of the legs as they keep the jumping character off the ground. There will be tension in the leg muscles and both of the feet should be flexed.

Drawing geometric shapes for each of the limbs and use circles to link them at the joints. Your sketch should now start to look three-dimensional.

Start with a basic structural sketch using pencil. Draw the legs as straight lines for now, and use geometric shapes for the hips and feet.

Use your guide to develop the shape of the legs to make them more realistic. The leg muscles are tense and the feet flexed.

67

Finish your initial sketch, giving more shape to the feet and defining each of the toes. Go over your drawing in ink. Erase any unwanted pencil lines.

Use pencil to draw in the character's shorts. These are tight-fitting and simply drawn using a couple lines across the mid-thigh area.

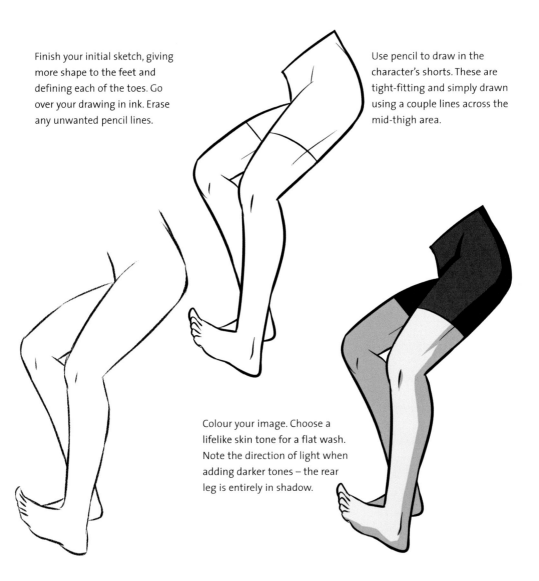

Colour your image. Choose a lifelike skin tone for a flat wash. Note the direction of light when adding darker tones – the rear leg is entirely in shadow.

DANCING

This pose is not dissimilar to the running pose on pages 65–66. It is reasonably straightforward in that the legs are seen face on and so are easier to draw.

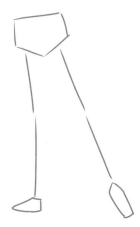

Start with a simple pencil sketch. Draw straight lines as guides for the legs, and geometric shapes for the hips and feet.

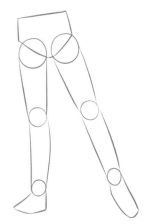

Draw the legs as geometric shapes now, linked at the joints by circles. Define the shapes of the feet better.

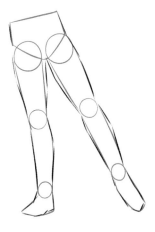

Use your guide to develop the shapes of the legs to make them more realistic. They are in tension and quite muscular.

Build up the muscles. First define your outline to show the thigh and calf muscles in profile beneath the skin.

Define the fronts of the legs better. Draw some lines to suggest the knee caps. These will help emphasise the muscles.

Draw in the tops of the thighs where they meet the pelvis. Add a few feint lines mid-thigh to suggest taut muscles.

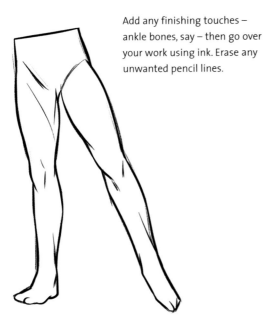

Add any finishing touches – ankle bones, say – then go over your work using ink. Erase any unwanted pencil lines.

Colour your image. Choose a lifelike skin tone for a flat wash. Use a darker tone in the areas that are in shadow.

Use pencil to draw in the dancer's shorts. They are tight-fitting. You need only draw an outline, which you can then go over using ink.

GALLERY

Here are a number of guides for drawing a range of different poses. The key to success is in getting the right proportions and perspective. As with other body parts, it is always a good idea to source a handful of visual references to help you.

rear view standing

right This is a pose you might use for someone standing leaning against a surface, helping to take the weight of the raised leg.

seated figure

below This character is sitting, perhaps halfway up a flight of stairs, with one foot resting on the step below.

walking

above A character walking, seen from the three-quarter view. You can adapt the foot front view on page 63 for drawing the feet.

skipping for joy

left This is quite a quirky, cheeky pose. Note the legs touching at the thighs and the lower limbs turned in.

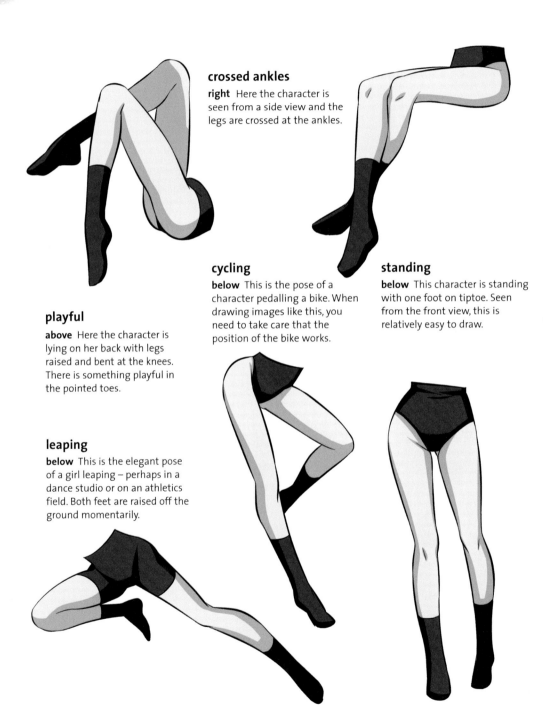

crossed ankles

right Here the character is seen from a side view and the legs are crossed at the ankles.

cycling

below This is the pose of a character pedalling a bike. When drawing images like this, you need to take care that the position of the bike works.

standing

below This character is standing with one foot on tiptoe. Seen from the front view, this is relatively easy to draw.

playful

above Here the character is lying on her back with legs raised and bent at the knees. There is something playful in the pointed toes.

leaping

below This is the elegant pose of a girl leaping – perhaps in a dance studio or on an athletics field. Both feet are raised off the ground momentarily.

GLOSSARY

compass A technical drawing instrument used for drawing arcs and circles.

drawing board A desk designed specifically for drawing.

feint A very fine drawn line, usually used as a guide.

felt-tip pen A pen with a tip made of porous, pressed fibers, often felt.

freehand Done without any mechanical aids or devices.

gouache A type of paint similar to watercolor that is heavier and opaque.

highlight A light spot or area in a painting used to emphasize light and shadow.

outline A first basic pencil sketch that helps with proportion before the art is completed.

perspective An art technique used to give the illusion of depth and distance.

putty eraser A type of eraser that can be kneaded and shaped and leaves less residue than rubber erasers.

sketch A fast freehand drawing.

tracing paper Translucent paper that, when laid over the top of a picture, allows the picture to show through, in order for it to be replicated.

watercolour A type of paint where pigment is suspended in water, resulting in a light color that allows the canvas to show through.

Animazing Gallery
54 Greene Street
New York, NY 10013
(212) 226-7374
Web site: http://www.animazing.com
Art gallery that exhibits a unique collection of original and
    limited edition animation and illustration artwork that
    indulges the senses and emotions with color and
    playfulness.

Japan Society
333 East 47th Street
New York, NY 10017
(212) 832-1155
Web site: http://www.japansociety.org
Japan Society is an American nonprofit organization that
    brings the people of Japan and the United States closer
    together through mutual understanding, appreciation,
    and cooperation.

Midtown Comics
200 W. 40th Street
New York, NY 10018
Web site: http://www.midtowncomics.com
Comic book store with a huge selection of manga that can
    be ordered online.

Midwest Comic Book Association
P.O. Box 131475

Saint Paul, MN 55113
(612) 237-1801
Web site: http://midwestcomicbook.com
This association organizes events where comic book
    enthusiasts and collectors can get together and share
    and trade their finds.

Museum of Comic and Cartoon Art
594 Broadway, Suite 401
New York, NY 10012
Web site: http://moccany.org
New York art gallery that features a large collection of
    comic book art.

Web Sites

Due to the changing nature of Internet links, Rosen
Publishing has developed an online list of Web sites related
to the subject of this book. This site is updated regularly.
Please use this link to access the list:

http://www.rosenlinks.com/MAMA/Faces

FOR FURTHER READING

Amberlyn, J.C. *Drawing Manga Animals, Chibis, and Other Adorable Creatures.* New York, NY: Watson-Guptill, 2009.

Bunyapen, Supittha. *Shojo Wonder Manga Art School: Create Your Own Cool Characters and Costumes with Markers.* Cincinnati, OH: IMPACT, 2011.

Casaus, Fernando. *The Monster Book of Manga: Draw Like the Experts.* New York, NY: HarperCollins, 2006.

Crilley, Mark. *Mastering Manga with Mark Crilley.* Cincinnati, OH: IMPACT, 2012.

Flores, Irene. *Shojo Fashion Manga Art School: How to Draw Cool Looks and Characters.* Cincinnati, OH: IMPACT, 2009.

Hart, Christopher. *Basic Anatomy for the Manga Artist: Everything You Need to Start Drawing Authentic Manga Characters.* New York, NY: Watson-Guptill, 2011.

Hart, Christopher. *Manga for the Beginner: Everything You Need to Start Drawing Right Away!* New York, NY: Watson-Guptill, 2008.

Hart, Christopher. *Manga for the Beginner Chibis: Everything You Need to Start Drawing the Super-Cute Characters of Japanese Comics.* New York, NY: Watson-Guptill, 2010.

Hart, Christopher. *Manga Mania Magical Girls and Friends: How to Draw the Super-Popular Action Fantasy Characters of Manga.* New York, NY: Watson-Guptill, 2006.

Hills, Doug. *Manga Studio for Dummies*. Hoboken, NJ: Wiley, 2008.

Ikari Studio, ed. *The Monster Book of Manga: Girls*. New York, NY: Harper Design, 2008.

Ikari Studio, ed. *The Monster Book of More Manga: Draw Like the Experts*. New York, NY: Harper Design, 2007.

INDEX

A

arm anatomy, 43
arms, hands, and fingers, drawing, 41–58
  arm anatomy, 43
  arms natural pose, 49–50
  fingers picking up, 48
  fist, 46
  gallery, 57–58
  lifting weights, 53–54
  open hand, 45
  open palm, 44
  painting nails, 51–52
  pointing finger, 47
  praying, 55–56

B

bodies and poses, drawing, 35–40
  gallery, 39–40
  seated female, 37–38

C

coloured pencils, 9–12
computer, working on a, 16–17

D

drawing aids, 14–15
drawing board, 15–16

E

erasers, 12–13
expressions and emotions, drawing, 18–24
  angry girl, 21
  annoyed man, 19
  evil expression, 22
  gallery, 23–24
  happy girl, 20

H

hairstyles, drawing, 25–34
  curly hair, 25–26
  black hair with highlights, 32
  blonde hair with highlights, 33
  gallery, 34
  highlights, 31, 32, 33
  ringlets, 27–28
  wavy hair, 29–30

I

inking pens, 13

L

leg anatomy, 61
legs, feet, and toes, drawing, 59–72
  dancing, 69–70
  foot from below, 64
  foot front view, 63

foot side view, 62
gallery, 71–72
jumping, 67–68
leg anatomy, 61
running, 65–66

M

mannequin, 16
markers and colouring aids, 14
materials and equipment to draw
    manga, 6–17

P

papers, 8–9
pencils, 9
    coloured, 9–12
pens, inking, 13

S

sharpeners, 12

About the Authors

Anna Southgate is an experienced writer and editor who has worked extensively for publishers of adult illustrated reference books. Her recent work has included art instruction books and providing the text for a series of six manga titles.

Yishan Li is a professional manga artist living in Edinburgh, Scotland. Her work has been published in the UK, United States, France, and Switzerland. Yishan has published many books on manga, and she also draws a monthly strip, *The Adventures of CGI*, for *CosmoGirl!*